AIRLINE MARK

Tupolev Tu-154

COLIN BALLANTINE

Dennis Briggs BD10 9NE (27) Jan 13th '99'

Copyright © 1995 by Colin Ballantine

First published in the UK in 1995
by Airlife Publishing Ltd.

British Library Cataloguing in Publication Data
A catalogue record for this book is available from the British Library

ISBN 1 85310 465 5

Typeset by Litho Link Ltd, Welshpool, Powys, Wales
Printed in Hong Kong

Airlife Publishing Ltd

101 Longden Road, Shrewsbury SY3 9EB

Introduction

The Tupolev Tu-154 was designed as a replacement for the Tupolev Tu-104 jet airliner and the Illyushin Il-18 turboprop airliner to operate medium haul routes within the former Soviet Union and in keeping with the Il-18, market the type as an export earner to existing Il-18 operators.

The design team was headed by Andrei Tupolev and his deputy Sergei Yeger who had been responsible for designs of the Tu-104, Tu-110, Tu-124 and Tu-134 jet airliners. When details were released in 1966 the drawings and specifications were comparable with the Boeing 727-200 although the Tu-154 is marginally bigger and faster; however, this was the turning point in Russian civil aviation to produce a comparable product with the West. The familiar glazed nose had gone and the Tu-154 was also the first Russian-built airliner to feature power-operated controls using Western components and technology.

The production line was set up at Kuibyshev with the prototype and pre-production models being transported to Zhukovskii, a test and research airfield on the south edge of Moscow's sprawling suburbs, for their first flight and subsequent flight testing for certification.

The prototype CCCP-85000 made its first flight in October 1968 with test pilot N. Goryanov in command. Testing and certification was completed by the summer of 1970 and Aeroflot took delivery of several aircraft during the latter part of 1970 for training and cargo flights while the prototypes continued to be evaluated in the hot and high areas of southern Russia and the frozen wastes of Siberia.

The first passenger services were inaugurated in November 1971 from Moscow-Vnukovo to Simferopol and Mineralnye Vody with the first international flights following in August 1972 between Moscow–Sheremetyevo and Prague-Ruzyne. During the next eight years, the Tu-154 achieved the purpose it was built for, to replace the Il-18 and Tu-104 airliners throughout Russian airspace.

The Tu-154 has been manufactured in six versions. The basic Tu-154 was designed as a 164-seat airliner of which 58 were built. Sixty-two Tu-154A versions then followed with up-graded Kuznetsov engines and an additional independent fuel tank not connected to the main system that was operated manually whilst on the ground. Next was the Tu-154B of which 107 examples were built featuring a lengthening of the cabin interior and another supplementary fuel tank. Avionics were up-graded in the next 70 examples resulting in the Tu-154B-1. The next version was the Tu-154B-2 which had the largest amount manufactured at 307 examples. It had another fuel capacity increase with all tanks connected to the main system with engine modifications and up-graded avionics compatible to Western standards. In 1984 the ultimate version came off the production line and was known as the Tu-154M. It was fitted with the reliable Soloviev D-30KU-154-II turbofan engines, had redesigned tail and engine nacelles to accommodate the more powerful motors and modifications to the wing slats and spoilers. The interior was also fine tuned to give that wide-body look.

As the early model Tu-154, Tu-154A and certain Tu-154B models are becoming due for major overhauls they are being up-graded to B-2 standard. At the time of writing production is very close to 800 examples of all versions.

Obviously the largest operator is the former Soviet Union territories with Aeroflot and the newly-formed Russian and C.I.S. airlines, however, at least 140 examples have been exported to 19 countries with Bulgaria as the largest export operator.

During 1992, I had the good fortune to fly on Tu-154Ms of Aeroflot and MIAT Mongolian Airlines; it was very impressive with quiet engines, cleanly fitted interiors and comfortable seating with plenty of leg room.

Despite Russia's eagerness to buy Western airliners, by sheer numbers the Tu-154 will be around well past the end of the twentieth century.

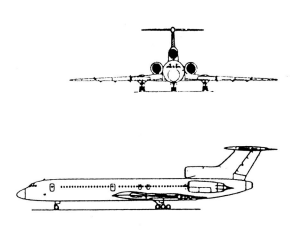
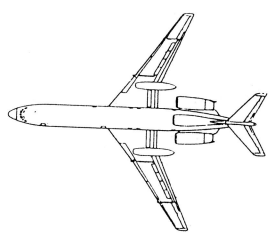

All photographs by Colin Ballantine, Tom Singfield, Hans Oehninger, Udo Schaefer and Christian Volpati.

AEROFLOT (SU/AFL)

Russia

Since the early post-war years, Aeroflot, during its growth has put heavy demands on the former Soviet Union's aviation manufacturers. With the enormous size of the Russian Federation and the Commonwealth of Independent States certain types of airliners have been produced in large numbers to cover air routes across this massive country.

The Tu-154 was evaluated as the combined Il-18 and Tu-104 replacement to operate medium and long haul routes within the Soviet Union and medium haul international flights for Aeroflot's requirements that now total an inventory of 700 plus Tu-154s, and into 1994 are still being built and accepted by Aeroflot.

The Moscow Transport Directorate of Aeroflot took delivery of its first Tu-154s in September 1970 for crew training and by May 1971 had started to operate a series of scheduled cargo and mail flights eastbound from Moscow-Novosibirsk-Irkutsk-Khabarovsk and southbound to Sochi and Simferopol. Full schedule passenger services were started in February 1972 from Moscow to Mineralnye Vody using a 152-seat layout. International services followed five months later in July 1972 on the Moscow-Berlin route and by the end of 1972 were a regular sight at Prague, Budapest and Sofia. The spring of 1973 saw regular Tu-154s operating flights into most airports in western Europe in a configuration of 12 first-class and 114 economy. July 1974 saw the first Tu-154 in a new colour scheme being CCCP-85058, also the first Tu-154A. By 1980 the Tu-154 had forced every Tu-104 into retirement and the Il-18s had been restricted to selected short haul flights within the Soviet Union.

As later model Tu-154s were delivered to Aeroflot with a superior range over early models, they were employed on longer all-Union routes and international routes as far away as east and west Africa and the Asian Far East with increased seating capacity. Into the 1990s the international Tu-154Ms are configured for 12 first-class, 18 business class and 102 economy and within Russia and the C.I.S. operate with 164 economy seats.

AEROFLOT (SU/AFL)

Russia

Aeroflot is responsible for all cargo operations and holds an enormous amount of freighters both jet and propeller-driven to support its freight network.

The Tu-154C is a newcomer to Aeroflot Cargo and replaces the Il-18 freighters on medium haul routes within the Russian Federation. At the time of writing a known eight Tu-154s have been converted from passenger versions to pure freighters with all examples being the older basic Tu-154 and Tu-154As. As older passenger versions become surplus more will go through the Aeroflot workshops for a new life as a freighter. All examples so far sighted can only be recognised by their cargo door as they do not carry the 'Aeroflot Cargo' titles.

Every principal airport in Russia plays host to the Tu-154 at least once a day and it is not uncommon to witness 100 different Tu-154s at Moscow's airports during the course of one day.

Several Tu-154Ms in Aeroflot colours are reserved for Government use as VIP transports based at Moscow-Vnukovo Airport: these airliners are fitted with additional communication equipment and lavishly appointed interiors.

The Tu-154 will take Aeroflot into the twenty-first century until replaced by the next generation of mass-produced Russian-built airliners.

AERONICA (RL/ANI)   Nicaragua

Nicaragua's civil aviation goes back to the days of Lanica who changed their identity in 1981 to Aeronica. The airline operated a piston-engined collection of DC-3s, DC-6s and C-46s until December 1989, when a new Tu-154M joined the fleet.

The smartly painted TU-154 named *Momotombo* operated unscheduled services around the Caribbean area. Aeronica is believed to have ceased as an airline with its passenger work being taken over by the Air Force. The Tu-154 was last reported laid up and rotting away at Managua.

AIR GREAT WALL (GW/CGW)   China

During October 1992 the CAAC Flying College at Guanghan in
Sichuan Province entered the commercial market from its new base
at Chongqing. Two Tu-154Ms were leased from Aeroflot to operate
tourist flights to Beijing, Xian and Guilin. Schedule flights were later
added to the airline's network covering services to Guangzhou,
Haikou, Harbin, Shanghai, Ningbo and Wenzhou.
   Currently B-2627 and B-2628 are the only two examples.

AIR KORYO (JS/KCA) North Korea

The Democratic People's Republic of Korea, known as North Korea, became a Republic with Soviet assistance in 1948. All civil and government air services were operated by Aeroflot until 1950 when the Soviet Union and North Korea formed a joint venture airline known as SOKOA that operated until 1956 with An-2, Il-12 and Li-2 aircraft. A restructure of the airline allowed North Korea to purchase the Soviet share of SOKOA and the name CAAK Civil Aviation Administration of Korea or locally known as UKAMPS was adopted. Il-14s joined the collection of veteran airliners on the sparse route network followed a few years later by the An-24s. In 1967, the Air Force took control of CAAK and converted it into a paramilitary airline using the name of Chosonminhang and operated under the control of the Air Force Transport Regiment. Selected aircraft were painted in the North Korean colours of red and white and continued to operate their small route network mainly to Peking, Moscow and Khabarovsk.

In 1975, the first of two Tu-154As were delivered to CAAK, the third a Tu-154B arrived in 1979 and the fourth example a Tu-154B-2 arrived in 1982. The first three aircraft 551/552/553 were delivered with CAAK titles but without the country's registration letter of 'P'. This is thought to have been added in the latter part of 1979. Initially the Tu-154s were used on the regular non-schedule flights to Berlin and later to Prague, then soon replaced the Il-18s on the prime route to Moscow via Irkutsk and Novosibirsk. Occasionally a Tu-154 would operate a government flight into the West with sightings in Tokyo, Stockholm, Paris, Geneva and even Harare. With the introduction of the Il-62, the Tu-154s are restricted to schedule flights twice weekly to Beijing and once weekly to Sofia via Moscow. The CAAK Tu-154s are considered a rare airliner in the Western world.

During 1992, CAAK added Air Koryo titles to their airliners and a tail logo.

AIR MOLDOVA (9U/MLD)

Moldavia

Moldavia is one of the smaller former Soviet states with a small and relatively prosperous population sharing its borders with Romania and Ukraine.

The national airline, Air Moldova currently operates nine Tu-134s and three Tu-154s from its capital base of Kishinev.

Although the Tu-154s have scheduled routes around the Black Sea areas, the airliners have appeared several times in Western Europe operating charters.

AIR UKRAINE (6U/UKR)   Ukraine

Ukraine is the largest of the former Soviet Republics and is stocked with a substantial aviation industry and airline.

Air Ukraine was established in 1992 as a domestic and international carrier from its two bases of Kiev-Borispol and Kiev-Zhulyany airports.

The Air Ukraine fleet currently consists of 90 airliners, Yk-40s, An-24s, An-26s, Tu-134s, Yk-24s, Il-62s and 22 Tu-154s, all of which now carry the full Air Ukraine markings and colours.

ALAK (J4/LSV)

Russia

As the mighty Aeroflot is gradually being dismantled several new independent airlines are emerging from Moscow.

ALAK is one such airline operating three Tu-154Ms from Moscow-Vnukovo airport to neighbouring cities in the Russian Federation.

ALYEMDA (DY/DYA)

South Yemen

South Yemen, formerly known as Aden, became independent in November 1967 from British rule and occupation. In 1969 the Soviet Union offered assistance in exchange for a Soviet Naval base, hence vast amounts of Soviet flying hardware poured into South Yemen. The Government in March 1971 established the airline, Alyemda with DC-3s and DC-6s for schedule services around the Middle East. A pair of Boeing 707s and three Dash Sevens also joined the fleet to support additional local routes.

During 1981, Alyemda took delivery of Tu-154B-2, 70-ACN in full airline colours. The airliner was first seen outside the Middle East region when in October 1981 it arrived at Berlin-Schonefeld Airport carrying a Government delegation on an official state visit. It was never established if 70-ACN was in normal passenger layout or a VIP interior, nor was it confirmed if it flew schedule flights. Alpha Charlie November carried a thin red line under the main cheatline of dark blue, registration on the engine covers and titles of Alyemda People's Democratic Republic of Yemen stretched along the entire length of the roof. A small white circle on the tail carried the country's colours of red, white and blue in the centre. The aircraft was never seen again outside of the Middle East and presumed sold back to the Soviet Union.

In August 1991, Tu-154M, 70-ACT visited Gatwick in full Alyemda colours somewhat different from the previous example.

Alpha Charlie Tango, operated by the South Yemen Government was reported to be in storage in Moscow, however recent reports state its new owner is Krai Aero.

ARIANA AFGHAN AIRLINES (FG/AFG)

Afghanistan

Ariana Afghan Airlines was founded in 1957 with Western help using DC-6 airliners. In 1973 the country moved to Communist rule and Soviet-built aircraft became the order of the day.

Since that year Ariana Afghan has operated the Yk-40 and An-24 airliners on domestic routes and not until 1987 did the airline take delivery of two Tu-154Ms for international routes to Amritsar, Delhi, Dubai, Moscow, Prague, Tashkent and Tehran.

ARMENIAN AIRLINES (R3/RME)   Armenia

Armenia is the smallest of all former Soviet states situated in a scenic area near the Turkish border.

Due to the Republics internal problems since Glastnost, the Government was forced to put the airlines future plans on hold, however, during 1993 Armenian Airlines was established as the national carrier and is now fully operational.

The fleet of ten Tu-154s operate regional services from their base at Yerevan, with occasional charters into Western Europe.

The Tu-154s carry titles of ARMENIA in English on the starboard side and Armenian script on the port side.

AVIAZNEGRO

Russia

Founded during 1994 from Moscow, Aviaznegro currently operates back-up schedules for Russian International Airlines with Tu-154s.

AZERBAIJAN AIRLINES (J2/AHY)   Azerbaijan

Azerbaijan was one of the three Trans-Caucasian republics separating Iran and Turkey from the former Soviet Union.

The Caucasus mountains form a natural border in the west near Erevan and in the east, Baku is the capital of Azerbaijan nestling on the shores of the Caspian Sea. The country is mountainous with a sparse road and rail system and depends heavily on air transport.

The oil rich state draws this valuable resource from the Caspian Sea with intense helicopter operations servicing the off-shore rigs.

Azerbaijan Airlines also operates Yk-40s, An-26s, Tu-134s and twelve Tu-154s as well as the recent leasing of two Boeing 727s.

The Tu-154s operate to Moscow and across the Caspian Sea to neighbouring Kazakhstan, Turkmenistan and Uzbekistan.

BALKAN (LZ/LAZ)   Bulgaria

In July 1947, the Bulgarian Government established the new national airline BVS-Bulgarshe Vazdusne Sobstenie to operate domestic routes only and using a small amount of Ju-52s and Li-2s until the airline lost its independence. It was in 1949 that the Soviet Union and Bulgaria formed a joint venture airline under a new civil aviation unit. The new airline known as TABSO stood for the initials of the Bulgarian-Soviet Joint Stock Company for Civil Aviation. The partnership lasted until 1954 when the Bulgarian Government purchased the Soviet Union's fifty per cent share. The name TABSO was retained: however, many aircraft used on international routes carried dual titles, the other being Bulgarian Air Transport. A charter division of TABSO known as Bulair was created in 1968 for inclusive tourist work to the Black Sea resorts of Varna and Bourgas using most of the TABSO/Bulgarian Air Transport Il-18 fleet during the summer months with Bulair titles applied to the forward fuselage.

In 1971 TABSO, Bulair and Bulgarian Air Transport were integrated into one state airline, Balkan as it is known today. The colour scheme of TABSO's blue was succeeded by Balkan's familiar red. Balkan is responsible for many other operations under the control of the Bulgarian Air Ministry, a system based on that of Aeroflot and Interflug with their industrial, agricultural and VIP transport divisions.

Since the Soviet involvement in 1949, Bulgaria has relied heavily on Soviet-built transport aircraft. International routes have been operated by Il-14, Il-18 and Tu-134 airliners, however, these have been phased out over the years in favour of the Tu-154 tri-jet.

Balkan was the first operator outside of the Soviet union to take delivery of the twenty-sixth production Tu-154 back in May 1972. Since then 30 Tu-154s have been delivered to Balkan who have used the airliners for 20 years on their prime international routes. All early model basic Tu-154s have been up-graded to Tu-154Bs and also operate B-1, B-2 and M versions. During 1976 and 1977 Balkan purchased three ex-Aeroflot basic Tu-154s whose previous identity was Egyptair: these three airliners were returned to the Soviet Union in exchange for B versions.

Currently Balkan utilises its Tu-154 fleet to Abu Dhabi, Algiers, Barcelona, Berlin, Casablanca, Colombo, Moscow, Paris and Tel Aviv. With the introduction of A-320 Airbuses, Boeing 737s and Boeing 767s, the Balkan Tu-154s are fast disappearing from many airports in Western Europe despite a new colour scheme to match the Western-built airliners.

BULGARIAN GOVERNMENT   Bulgaria

Tu-154B-1, LZ-BTJ was purchased in 1978 as their VIP transport for
the President and Government Ministers. The aircraft was rarely
seen outside of the Eastern Bloc countries during its twelve years as
a VIP airliner. The colours were similar to the Balkan Airlines' red
colour scheme, however, it was easily recognisable by its
Government coat-of-arms in the form of a circular badge behind the
cockpit windows on each side. Tango Juliet was transferred to
Balkan Airlines as an economy class passenger airliner in 1990
having been replaced with Tu-154M, LZ-BTZ as the Government
airliner.

BELAVIA (B2/BRU)   Belarus

During 1992, the former Soviet Republic of Belarus launched its new
aviation structure of Belavia using Yk-40s, An-24s, An-26s, Tu-134s
and a known twenty Tu-154s.

From the state's capital of Minsk, halfway between Warsaw and
Moscow, Belavia operates north to the three Baltic states and St.
Petersburg, south to the Ukraine and east to Moscow. The airline
has plans to operate the Tu-154 into Western Europe on schedule
services.

CAIRO CHARTER and CARGO (CJ/CCE)

Egypt

Cairo Air Transport Company was founded in 1991 as a charter freight operator from their base at Cairo International Airport. Currently the new airline operates two Ilyushin Il-76 freighters and two Tu-154M for passenger work.

C.A.A.C.

China

The original CAAC dates back to 1939 when the Sino-Soviet airline known as Hamiata established limited air services from Peking to Alma Ata under the direction of the Soviet Union. In 1952 the Soviet Union reviewed their co-operation with China which resulted in Skoga-People's Aviation Corporation of China being formed as a joint Chinese-Soviet venture. At the same time China established their own wholly-owned airline, China Civil Aviation Corporation. The Soviet Union withdrew from Skoga in 1954 and the Chinese merged both companies to form the present-day CAAC-China Civil Aviation Administration of China.

At the time of the inauguration of CAAC's early services under the new name, the fleet consisted mainly of An-2s, Il-12s and Li-2s that were supplemented in 1959 by Il-14s and in 1962 by Il-18s and An-24s.

During the 1960s relations with the Soviet Union deteriorated and many Western-built airliners were evaluated. The end result was Viscounts, Tridents and Boeing 707s being purchased to operate alongside a huge fleet of Soviet-built airliners. CAAC established several long haul international routes with the Boeing 707 carrying the airline into the Western world.

Ten Il-62s were ordered, but only five were delivered as CAAC cancelled their option on the remaining five due to information not being forthcoming from the Soviet Union regarding two serious accidents with the type during 1972. Boeing 747SPs were delivered to supplement the Boeing 707s on long haul routes and the Il-62 was quickly relegated to long haul routes within China as well as being obligated to use the airliners on the Peking-Moscow and Peking-Bucharest routes. During the 1980s, CAAC ordered more British, French and American airliners as part of their modernisation programme. However, with the thawing of Soviet-Chinese relations in 1986 the first of at least 30 Tu-154Ms were delivered over a three year period. Two years earlier, the Department of International Affairs within CAAC was broken up to create regional airlines within China with their own identity based on Western business principles. The Tu-154M fitted into the re-shaping programme perfectly and most of the early deliveries of the airliner were in full CAAC colours operating regional routes for their regional carrier. As the Tu-154Ms become due for overhaul they are being repainted into their regional carrier colours.

CHINA NORTHWEST (WH/CNW)   China

China Northwest, one of the big eight airlines in China was established in 1989 from its base in the ancient and historic city of Xian, Shaanxi Province.

Currently the airline operates 37 airliners comprising Y-7s, BAE-146s, A300/A310 Airbuses and 10 Tu-154Ms. Like the other Chinese Tu-154M operators, their schedule services cover the main tourist areas of Beijing, Changsha, Chongqing, Fuzhou, Guangzhou, Guilin, Haikou, Harbin, Lanzhou, Shanghai, Shanton, Shenyang, Shenzhen, Urumqi, Wenzhou and Xiamen.

CHINA SOUTHWEST AIRLINES (SZ/CXN)   China

Established in 1987 as China Southwest Airlines from the former
CAAC Chengdu Region. The airline operates five Tu-154Ms in the
brightest colour scheme yet seen on Chinese airliners from their
base at Chengdu and Chongquin. The Tu-154M routes radiate from
Chengdu to Beijing, Changchun, Changsha, Dalian, Fuzhou,
Guangzhou, Haikou, Shenyang, Urumqi and Xiamen.

CHINA UNITED AIRLINES (CUA)   China

In the 1984 CAAC reorganisation the Chinese Air Force was authorised to operate Government and Military flights based on revenue, not subsidies. The division became known as China United Airlines operating both passenger and cargo flights. The airline controls a wide variety of aircraft including Canadair Challengers for VIP use, An-24s, Y-7s, Boeing 737s, Il-76 freighters and fifteen Tu-154Ms. This unusual airline operates from the heavily wooded fortress base of Nan Yuan in the Beijing area.

One of the Tu-154Ms, B-4138 is used exclusively for China's top three heads of state in a VIP configuration and extensively modified with additional communication equipment. The remainder of the fleet are fitted with a 160-seat economy type layout for military and government groups flying within China.

The basic colours of the fleet are similar to the original CAAC, however, during 1992, CUA purchased three Tu-154Ms from CSA-Czechoslovak Airlines and currently fly in CUA markings with the CSA red tail and cheatline.

Generally regarded as the rarest Tu-154s to be sighted, the fleet normally operate from their base to other Chinese Air Force bases and are rarely seen at civilian airports in China.

CHINA XINJIANG AIRLINES (XO/CXJ)   China

China Xinjiang Airlines is thought to be one of the first regional
airlines to be established after the dismantling of CAAC in 1984.
China Xinjiang whose base is at Urumqi in the Xinjiang Province
operates and owns five Tu-154M and two leased from Aeroflot on
routes from Urumqi to Beijing, Chengdu, Dalian, Fuzhou, Guangzhou, Hangzhou, Harbin, Kashi, Lanzhou, Shanghai, Xiamen, Xian
and Zhengzhou. The airline also operates two international routes,
one to Alma Ata with the Tu-154M and the newly established Il-86
route to Moscow.

CSA CESKOSLOVENSKE AEROLINIE (OK/CSA)

Czech Republic

The former Czechoslovakia, like Poland and Hungary have been big Russian-built airliner operators since 1946. Li-2s, Il-12s, Il-14s and Il-18s have come and gone and are currently being followed by Yk-40s, Tu-134s and the Il-62s.

Since the delivery of the first Il-62 in 1969, CSA Ceskoslovenske Aerolinie adopted their two letter IATA code 'OK' into their familiar red and white colour scheme. The livery was carried over to fit the Tu-134s, Yk-40s, L-410 Turbolets and finally to the last two Il-18s.

In 1988, CSA took delivery of the first of seven Tu-154Ms in the OK jet colours in a configuration of 28 first-class and 136 economy class layout. The Tu-154Ms were pressed into service to replace the first five basic model Il-62s that were at the time averaging eighteen years old on European and Middle East routes. Initially the Tu-154s operate most of CSA's international routes. Not long after the first Boeing 737s arrived the Tu-154s were displaced off the European routes, operating only as a back-up or the occasional charter. The Tu-154 fleet then settled into the areas of Abidjan, Abu Dhabi, Beirut, Damascus, Kuwait, Moscow, Riga, St. Petersburg and Tel Aviv. As more B-737s arrive even these routes will be taken away from the Tu-154 and made surplus for disposal.

CSA CESKOSLOVENSKE AEROLINIE (OK/CSA)

Czech Republic

A new colour scheme was adopted in early 1991 to coincide with the purchase of two A-310 Airbuses. As the Tu-154Ms become due for overhaul they will be painted in the new colours as has happened with some examples. The charter work has all but dried up for the Czech Tu-154Ms and already they face an uncertain future with three examples having been sold to China United Airlines.

CUBANA (CU/CUB)

Cuba

The Compania Cubana de Aviacion began the island's domestic air services in 1930 with Ford Tri-motors. International services were initiated in 1946 with C-46, DC-3, DC-4 and Lockheed Constellation airliners. In 1959 the Castro Government embarked on a Communist system only to find himself cut off from the Western world that made the task of maintenance on airliners very difficult without spares. The Western type airliners were quickly disposed of and replaced with a large fleet of Soviet-built airliners that have served Cubana well for the past three decades.

The Tu-154 was chosen as the replacement for the Il-18. Five Tu-154B-2s were delivered, one per year between 1980 and 1984, followed by three Tu-154Ms again one per year between 1986 and 1988. Cubana also bought the sole example Tu-154M from Guyana Airways Corporation thus making the Tu-154 fleet nine aircraft.

Cubana uses the Tu-154s mainly on the Havana-Montreal, Havana-Mexico City routes and covers the charter work within their range.

CZECHOSLOVAK GOVERNMENT FLYING SERVICE – LSFMV

The former LOFMV, now currently known as the LSFMV, is basically the Czechoslovak Government's own airline responsible for VIP and Government delegation flights. Since inception in 1947 the LSFMV have operated an impressive array of aircraft in their own colour scheme from their own base at Prague-Ruzyne Airport. The fleet is classified by registrations in the OK-Bravo Yankee series from Alpha to Zulu.

The first two aircraft commissioned were an Avia-S199 being a licence-built Messerschmitt BF-109 and a Mraz K-65 Cap being a licence-built Fieseler Fi-156 Storch. Both aircraft served the LSFMV until 1956 when they were retired to Prague-Kbely Museum. The Mi-1 and Mi-4 helicopters kept the fleet alive until the arrival of five Il-14s (Avia-14 versions). Two Il-18s then joined the fleet followed by four Tu-134As, eight Yk-40s, two Il-62s and now the latest acquisition of six Tu-154s.

The first four examples of OK-BYA/B/C/D are Tu-154B-2s, with OK-BYA being delivered in 1980 and the last OK-BYD arriving in 1985. In May 1989, Tu-154M OK-BYO arrived followed by OK-BYP in January 1991 wearing a non-standard colour scheme registered to the LSFMV.

With the collapse of the Soviet Empire, Czechoslovakian aviation authorities were quick to dispense with seldom-used airliners. Yankee Alpha with its 96-seat VIP interior went to the Czech Air Force as did Yankee Delta. Yankee Charlie was re-registered OK-LCS and operated a short time for Cargo Moravia and Yankee Bravo was re-registered OK-LCP with Ensor Air. Currently two Tu-154Ms are still with the LSFMV operating in their attractive red and white untitled livery with the triangular version of the national roundel on the tail.

CZECHOSLOVAK AIR FORCE

Since the mid 1950s the Czechoslovak Air Force has operated 51 Avia-14s for general purpose transport duties, only two were known to be VIP versions. These two aircraft were superseded by a VIP Tu-134A 1407 which has been the solo Air Force VIP transport since 1971 and is still active with low hours.

In April 1989, the VIP division of the transport regiment of the Czechoslovak Air Force took delivery of the LSFMV Tu-154B-2 OK-BYA as 0420. Still in the LSFMV colours the registration is carried on the engine covers and the triangular national roundel has been replaced by the normal circular roundel applied to Air Force registered aircraft.

Again surplus to requirements from the LSFMV fleet OK-BYD was transferred to the Air Force in February 1991 as 0601. This aircraft was re-fitted and carries a ventral fin on the roof containing specialised communication equipment. On each side of the front end behind the cockpit windows the aircraft bears a large coat-of-arms of Czechoslovakia and Slovenia. Above the front row of cabin windows the titles Czechoslovak Air Force stand out in grey against a white background and the aircraft is finished in an attractive red and blue cheatline from under the nose along the fuselage and sweeping up to the base of the rudder. Engine covers are blue with 0601 in white on the side of the covers. 0601 is based at Prague-Kbely and is a smart example of an Air Force VIP transport.

DAALLO AIRLINES
Djibouti

This small former French colony is located on the Horn of Africa facing Yemen at the foot of the Red Sea. In the past the country's airliners have been supplied by France; however, since 1991, Djibouti has taken an independent course and established a new supply from eastern Europe and Russia.

Daallo Airlines was founded in 1992 with a single leased L-410 Turbolet from Poland. Towards the end of 1993, the airline leased a Tu-154M from Aeroflot for non-scheduled passenger operations. The airliner operates from its two bases of Djibouti City and Sharjah, UAE.

EGYPTAIR (MS/MSR)   Egypt

Egypt's association with Russian-built airliners has been far from successful. The involvement started in 1965 with Misrair taking delivery of ten Antonov An-24s and in 1968 United Arab Airlines purchased four Ilyushin Il-18s. Misrair and United Arab Airlines then merged to form Egyptair who leased eight Ilyushin Il-62s until the delivery of eight Tu-154s. During the eight-year period from 1965 to 1973 eight An-24s were lost in accidents together with two Il-18s and one Il-62.

Six of the eight basic model Tu-154s were delivered from Kuybyshev to Leningrad, then to London-Heathrow where they were fitted out with British-made seats. SU-AXB was the first to arrive on 1 December 1973 and the last, SU-AXI left Heathrow in March 1974. Crew training took place on proving flights from Cairo to Moscow, Berlin, Prague and Dubai. On 10 July 1974, SU-AXB whilst performing touch-and-go landings at Cairo stalled at 1000 feet and crashed only a few miles from the airport. The remaining seven Tu-154s were immediately withdrawn from use and returned to the Soviet Union.

ENSOR AIR (E9/ENR)   *Czech Republic*

Ensor Air was established in 1992 as a charter operator and travel agency based in Prague.

OK-BYB from the Government fleet was purchased by Ensor Air as OK-LCP. The airliner had no charter contracts and was subsequently used by Exocel, a steel broker and part of the Vitkovice Steel Group. The arrangement was short-lived and Ensor Air sold OK-LCP to Aeroflot as RA-85488.

Ensor Air then purchased Tu-154M OK-BYP from the Government fleet as OK-VCP. Charlie Papa did operate a few charters on behalf of CSA to Middle East destinations, but regrettably this private operator has suspended operations whilst a new financial structure is developed. Into 1994 the airline is still active in a depressed passenger market in the Czech Republic.

ESTONIAN AIR (OV/ELL)   Estonia

Estonian Air was officially formed for airline operations in October 1991 as the national carrier of the Republic of Estonia from its Tallinn base.

The airline's fleet consists of Yk-40s and Tu-134s. The two Tu-154s depicted in their striking new blue colours provide services to Moscow and the neighbouring Baltic Republics.

EXPERIMENTAL Tu-154   Russia

During the mid 1980s, CCCP-85035 was withdrawn from the Aeroflot
fleet and sent to the experimental and test airfield of Zhukovsky
near Moscow.

The airliner was fitted with three highly modified engines and a
new fuel system to feed the engines CNG-Compressed Natural Gas
and LPG-Liquid Petroleum Gas. The results have never been
released; however, the airliner is known as the Tu-155 prototype.

GREENAIR (WK/GRN)   Turkey

Greenair was established in 1990 as a charter passenger operator from their base at Istanbul. The company leased two Tu-134A-3s and three Tu-154Ms from Aeroflot carrying the full colours of Greenair. The Tu-154Ms are named TC-GRA *Cappadocia*, TC-GRB *Perestroika* and TC-GRC *Fenerbahce*.

GUYANA AIRWAYS CORPORATION (GY/GYA)

Guyana

The former British colony of British Guiana, wedged between Venezuela and Surinam became independent in 1963 under its current name of Guyana. The national airline, Guyana Airways Corporation was established the same year with a few C-47 Dakotas that were later replaced with HS-748s.

In June 1984, Guyana Airways leased an Aeroflot Il-62M in full Guyana colours in an ambitious attempts to become a long distance international airline. The project failed and the Il-62M was returned to Aeroflot. A second attempt was made in January 1985 when Guyana Airways leased a Tarom Tu-154B-2 YR-TPK in full Guyana colours followed a few months later by YR-TPJ. Both aircraft were used around the Caribbean area as far as Miami. By March 1986 Guyana Airways had returned both airliners and purchased their own new Tu-154M as 8R-GGA. Spares became a problem being so far from the Soviet Union and nearby Cubana needed their own stocks for their Tu-154 fleet. The sole example was sold to Cubana as CU-T1276 in December 1988 and the airline continued the regional routes with their only Boeing 707.

INTERFLUG (IF/IFL)   East Germany

Interflug, formerly known as Deutsche Lufthansa was born out of a divided Germany in May 1954. Being part of the Eastern Bloc, substantial assistance was given by the former Soviet Union and of course all aircraft registered in the German Democratic Republic were Soviet built.

Interflug, like CSA and LOT, waited until the new Tu-154M was available for delivery to replace the early model and ageing Il-62s and Tu-134s.

The first of the Tu-154Ms, DDR-AFA was handed over to Interflug in May 1989 with DDR-AFB arriving at Schonefeld in September 1989. Both airliners did not have enough time to establish

themselves in the Interflug fleet and less than one month after Fox Bravo arrived, down came the Berlin Wall in October 1989. Most of the Interflug fleet were grounded as soon as Lufthansa took control.

Interflug ceased operations as the state airline of the German Democratic Republic on 30 April 1991 and the two Tu-154Ms were transferred to the Transport Wing of the Luftwaffe some months prior in October 1990.

Very few pictures exist of the Interflug Tu-154Ms because of their short stay with Interflug, however, it is quite likely with their seating layout that they were destined for Government use in Interflug colours as happened with certain Il-62s and Tu-134s.

KAZAKHSTAN AERO SERVICE (AVZ) Kazakhstan

Locally known as Kazakhstan Avia Kompanias, the airline was established during the latter part of 1993 as a second carrier of Kazakhstan.

The striking colour scheme is carried on two Tu-154s and one An-26 operating from its Alma Ata base.

KAZAKHSTAN AIRLINES (K4/KZA)   Kazakhstan

Kazakhstan Airlines operates from its base at Alma Ata in what was known as the former Soviet Union's second largest Republic.

The state's climate is varied from severe winters in the north to hot dry summers in the south thus justifying a wide variety of aircraft from An-2s to Il-76s.

The Tu-154 fleet is fairly small at the time of writing, however, but as more Aeroflot Tu-154s become due for overhaul the fleet size will increase.

Passenger services operated by the Tu-154 radiate to all neighbouring states and further to Moscow, Khabarovsk and Urumqi, China.

KRAJ AERO (K3/KIO)   Russia

During 1993, the redundant Alyemda Tu-154M was taken over by a
new Moscow operator, Krai Aero. The new company operates from
Moscow-Vnukovo airport.

KYRGYZSTAN AIRLINES (K2/KGA)   Kyrgyzstan

The Republic of Kyrgyzstan is situated between Kazakstan and the north-west China border in the mountainous region of central Asia.

Kyrgyzstan Airlines currently operate thirteen Tu-154s from their base at Bishkek. Flights to neighbouring former Soviet states are fully established, however, owing to the remote location the airliners are rarely seen in the western areas of Russia or outside Russia.

The airlines titles are Kirghiz language script displayed on both sides of the airliner.

LAOS AVIATION (QV/LAO)

Laos

Whilst Laos Aviation was awaiting a leased Boeing 737, the airline took a short term lease, believed to have been six months, from Balkan using a Tu-154. The airliner was used on the once-weekly service Vientiane-Bangkok route and rarely seen anywhere else. LZ-BTN was returned to Balkan in March 1992.

LATVIAN AIRLINES (PV/LTL)   Latvia

Based in one of the three Baltic Republics to break away from the Soviet Union, Latvian Airlines organised themselves into the national airline of the Republic of Latvia from their base at Riga during October 1991.

Latvian Airlines is the largest airline of the Baltic Republics and currently operates 18 helicopters and 70 airliners comprising An-2s, An-24s, An-26s, Tu-134s and eight Tu-154s.

Latvian Airlines radiate their flights from Riga to Copenhagen, Helsinki, Moscow, St. Petersburg, Simferopol, Sochi, Volgograd and Voronzeh.

LIBYAN ARAB AIRLINES (LN/LAA)   Libya

Libyan Arab Airlines leased six Balkan Tu-154s in November 1977 for the annual pilgrimage of Hadj flights to Mecca . . . only five returned. Two airliners were painted in full Libyan Arab Airlines colours of gold. On 2 December 1977, LZ-BTN was returning from Jeddah to Tripoli when it ran out of fuel near Labrak, Libya. A forced landing was attempted in the desert resulting in a total write-off of the airliner and 59 fatalities. This airliner was a basic Tu-154 previous owned by Egyptair. The registration was re-issued to LZ-BTN in 1990 being a Tu-154M.

LIETUVA (TT/KLA)

Latvia

Lietuva, also known as Air Lithuania was established in 1991
basically as the regional Lithuanian carrier using leased Yak-40s
and Tu-134s from the international carrier Lithuanian Airlines.
Operating from its base at Kanuas in central Lithuania, the airline
took delivery of its first leased Tu-154 from Aeroflot bearing the
company's full Lietuva colours. The Tu-154M will be used mainly on
scheduled services within the former Soviet Union and any
international charters that may occur.

LOT POLSKIE LINIE LOTNICZE (LO/LOT)

Poland

Poland's two private enterprise airlines of Aerolot and Aero T.Z. were formed in 1922 basically as domestic carriers with two international routes to Prague and Vienna. Both companies survived until December 1928 when they were taken over by the Polish Government and merged into the present day Polskie Linie Lotnicze. The inaugural LOT service took place in January 1929 with a fleet comprising German- and Dutch-built airliners and by 1939 LOT had developed routes to London, Copenhagen, Helsinki, Baghdad, Moscow and all cities of the former Eastern Bloc.

LOT ceased operations in 1940 after the German invasion and restarted in December 1945 after being repatriated by the Soviet Union. The airline was given a small supply of Li-2 airliners as a goodwill gesture to get the airline up and running. LOT fell out of favour with the Soviet authorities when they accepted C-47s from the West followed by five Convair 240s and three Viscounts to operate alongside the fleet of Il-14s. As the Western types became due for replacement they were followed by more Soviet-built airliners, An-24s, Il-18s, Tu-134s and Il-62s.

LOT, like CSA, waited until the Tu-154M was fully developed; however, as an interim measure two Tu-154B-2s were leased from Aeroflot with both examples being returned when the first Tu-154Ms were delivered.

The 154 fleet immediately replaced the Tu-134s on the dense medium-haul routes into Europe and the Il-62s into the Middle East; however, with the introduction of the LOT Boeing 737s and 767s, the Tu-154Ms are now restricted to the Middle East destinations of Abu Dhabi, Cairo, Damascus, Dubai, Istanbul, Larnaca, Tel Aviv and still operate the route to Moscow.

LOT/AEROFLOT LEASES (LO/LOT)   Hungary

As an evaluation programme, LOT leased two Tu-154Bs from
Aeroflot pending the delivery of their own Tu-154Ms of which
fourteen examples were ordered and delivered. The lease
commenced in June 1985 and terminated in June 1986 when the first
LOT Tu-154M was delivered. The two leased airliners, CCCP-85331
and CCCP-85455 were normal Aeroflot examples with the additional
titles of 'Chartered by LOT Polish Airlines'; however, at the end of
the lease period, CCCP-85455 was painted in full LOT colours and
re-leased until June 1987.

LUFTWAFFE

Germany

The German Luftwaffe inherited three Tu-134s, three Il-62s and two Tu-154Ms in October 1990 after the collapse of communist East Germany.

The Soviet-built VIP transports operated with Transport Group 44 of the East German Air Force and upon reunification were organised into a new Luftwaffe unit known as Lufttransport-geschwader 65 (LTG 65) based at Neuhardenburg, formerly known as Marxwalde.

The two Tu-154Ms with their Western avionics were cleared quickly to operate into the West, in fact, as soon as they were integrated into the Luftwaffe they were used as strategic transports for troops airlifted to Turkey in support of the Bundeswehr's involvement in Operation Desert Storm. Both have since visited the West as a support aircraft for the Luftwaffe's Russian component at air shows.

The need for transport aircraft between Berlin and Bonn has been extremely high since reunification and the future of the Tu-154Ms is assured in the short-term policy; however, when the Government has completed the restructure programme for the country the Soviet-built airliners of LTG 65 face an uncertain future.

MACEDONIA AIR SERVICES
(M2/MDO)

Macedonia Air Services was founded in the spring of 1992 as a holiday charter airline operating from its base at Skopje, capital of Macedonia. The airline operates two Tu-154Ms leased from Air VIA of Bulgaria.

MALEV (MA/MAH)   Hungary

The original Malev was founded in 1922 as MALERT (Magyar Legiforgalani) using German and Italian airliners, operating successfully until 1940. The airline emerged again in 1946 as Maszovlet, a joint Hungarian/Soviet venture using Li-2s that lasted until 1954 when the Hungarian Government purchased the 50 per cent Soviet share and established its own national identity as MALEV.

Under this independent agreement Malev was contracted to purchase Soviet-built airliners. The Li-2s were replaced by Il-14s followed by Il-18s, Tu-134s and in 1973 the Tu-154 arrived.

Malev took delivery of three basic Tu-154s and two Tu-154Bs, all of which were later converted to Tu-154B-2s to conform with their later deliveries of the B-2s currently totalling 12 aircraft. Malev operated another six Tu-154s two of which were lost in accidents and the other four were returned to Russia in exchange for B-2 models. A few early Tu-154s were delivered with an eight-seat first-class section and 143 economy seats, however, due to poor patronage and standardisation the fleet soon reverted back to the usual 149 seats.

Throughout the 1970s and 1980s the Tu-154s of Malev were a familiar sight around the airports of Europe; however, into the 1990s they are becoming elusive with their routes restricted to Kiev, Moscow and the Middle East cities of Beirut, Cairo, Damascus, Dubai, Kuwait, Lanarca and Tel Aviv and occasionally they operate charters. With the arrival of the newly-acquired Boeing 737s and Boeing 767s, the Tu-154s' days are numbered with the Hungarian flag carrier.

MALEV (MA/MAH)   Hungary

In 1989, Malev adopted a new colour scheme designed for the
Boeing 737. The colours were also applied to the remaining Tu-134s
and to the entire Tu-154 fleet as they became due for maintenance
work.

MALEV CARGO (MA/MAH)   Hungary

As the Malev Il-18s became due for replacement an early model Tu-154 was selected for conversion to the cargo division of Malev. HA-LCA was the first basic Tu-154 delivered in 1973, ten years later it was modified to a Tu-154B-2 and in 1992 was fully converted to a Tu-154S freighter.

The conversion is simple with the fitting of a roller bed floor and floor clips to secure the nine PAV-3 pallet base containers compatible with the aircraft. On the port side of the aircraft behind the cockpit is fitted a power-operated cargo door measuring 280 cm wide by 187 cm high through which the fuselage can accommodate a maximum of 19,000 kg or 135 cubic metres. Two under-floor holds can take 38 cubic metres that are seldom used if the main deck is full. The Tu-154S has a maximum range of 2800 km with a full load.

META AVIOTRANSPORT
MACEDONIA (MAM) (M5/MAM)

Macedonia

Meta Aviotransport was founded in the spring of 1992 as a holiday charter airline operating from its base at Ohrid. Currently two Tu-154Ms are leased from Aeroflot wearing MAM's smart new colours.

MONGOLIAN AIRLINES (OM/MGL)   Mongolia

Since the collapse of the Soviet Empire, countries such as Mongolia who relied heavily on Soviet support have struggled to survive. The airline is a perfect example, suffering from lack of spares and a severe fuel shortage.

To maintain the Beijing-Ulan Bator-Moscow route, Mongolian Airlines had to lease a Tu-154B-2 from Aeroflot between 1988-1990, when it was replaced with a later model Tu-154M that is still current.

ORBI (NQ/DVU)

Georgia

ORBI Georgian Airways was founded in 1992 as an independent airline operating from the country's capital of Tbilisi.

The private airline operates Tu-134s to nearby Batumi and Sochi on schedule services, whilst the Tu-154s cover Moscow and St. Petersburg. ORBI also have international rights to Cairo, Tel Aviv, Thessaloniki and Vienna.

PALAIR MACEDONIAN (3D-PMK)   Macedonia

During 1991, Palair Macedonian was established by the Macedonian leisure group Paltourist & Palprint to operate package holiday charters from its Skopje base. The airline's two Tu-154Ms are leased from Balkan in full Palair Macedonian colours.

POLISH AIR FORCE

Poland

The Polish Air Force has always operated a substantial amount of VIP transports, Il-14s, Il-18s, Tu-134s, Yk-40s and in 1990 took delivery of a new Tu-154M for Air Force and Government use. 837 is the sole example operating from its base at Warsaw-Okecie Airport.

SICHUAN AIRLINES (3U/CSC)   China

Sichuan Airlines was established in 1986 from its base at Chengdu in Sichuan Province. For the first six years the airline operated four Chinese-built Y7-100 turbo-prop airliners. During 1992, the airline secured enough funding to finance the purchase of four Tu-154Ms.

From Chengdu the jet services are currently flying to the valuable tourist centres of Beijing, Changsha, Chongqing, Guangzhou, Guilin, Guiyang, Wanxian, Wuhan and Xian.

SYRIANAIR (RB/SYR)   Syria

Since 1955, the Government of Syria has authorised the purchase of large amounts of Soviet flying hardware that has spilt over into the national airline. Some early model An-24s, An-26s and Yk-40s are still serving the airline on local Government and domestic flights. The Tu-134B-3s were delivered in full airline colours in 1982 and 1983, followed by three Tu-154Ms in 1985. These smart-looking airliners in full colours are restricted on routes to Moscow, Dhahran, Algeries, Tunis and operate the odd charter to remote destinations. Occasionally they substitute for a Tu-134B-3, but generally speaking they are fairly rare airliners to be seen.

TAROM (RO/ROT)

Romania

Since the early post-war years of 1946 when Tarom was founded, the airline has been a big user of Russian-built airliners. Starting with a 24-strong fleet of Lisunov Li-2s, operating under their original name of TARS-Transporturi Aeriene Romano-Sovietice, the airline progressed to Il-14s, An-24s, Il-18s, Il-62s and finally the Tu-154.

A fleet of 12 Tu-154B, B-1 and B-2 versions were delivered between 1976 and 1980 to replace the Il-18s on schedule and charter flights. Four have been lost in accidents and with the invasion of A-310 Airbuses and Boeing 737s, the Tu-154s now face a short future.

TOJIKAIR (7J/TAK) Tajikistan

This small independent state shares its borders with China, Afghanistan, Uzbekistan and Kyrgystan. The recently-established airline operates from its capital of Dushanbe using a variety of An-24, An-26, Tu-134, Tu-154, Yk-40 and Yk-42 airliners. The three Tu-154s are the flag carriers to its neighbouring states and Moscow.

TRANSAIR MALI (FA/TSM)

Mali

During 1990, the aviation structure in the Republic of Mali collapsed leaving the state without an international airline. Transair Mali was established in 1991 with the help of Aeroflot's leasing division resulting in a single Tu-154M operating unscheduled services to Paris and neighbouring African countries. The Tu-154M is still current and has been joined by an An-12 freighter.

TUPOLEV FACTORY PROTOTYPES   Russia

The first five Tu-154s are believed to be genuine prototypes, being CCCP-85000/1/2/3/4. All examples were painted in full original Aeroflot colours. The first airliner CCCP-85000 was displayed at the 1969 Paris Air Show and went on to become the prime testing airliner for the large production which followed.

TURKMENAVIA (TS/TUA)

Turkmenistan

Turkmenistan National State Aviacompany known in its shortened form as Turkmenavia has emerged from Aeroflot as one of the most wealthy air operators in the former Soviet Union.

From its base at Ashkhabad, the Government operated the two Tu-154s, initially on passenger schedules and later as VIP transports. These operations were short-lived and both airliners were replaced with a HS-125-1000, a Boeing 737-400 and more recently a Boeing 747SP, all paid for from the proceeds of the oil-rich state.

The airline currently has on hand four Tu-154s for schedule services to Moscow and the neighbouring states of Kazahstan, Uzbekistan and Tajikistan with more schedules planned for 1994.

UZBEKISTAN AIRWAYS (HY/UZB)

C.I.S.

Uzbekistan is one of the Muslim provinces making up the nine Commonwealth of Independent States. Being somewhat isolated in the south central part of the former Soviet Union it was no surprise that Uzbekistan formed a fairly substantial airline in 1991 under its own identity of Uzbekistan Airways. From their base at Tashkent, the airline has inherited the Il-62 maintenance facility and quickly purchased six of the ex-Interflug Il-62Ms returned to Tashkent upon the collapse of Interflug. A fleet of Tu-154Ms has started to appear to provide air links to the neighbouring C.I.S. provinces and further afield to cities in the Russian Federation.

VARDAR BOSNAAIR (VB/BAA)   Macedonia

Originally established in 1992 as a holiday charter airline, Bosnaair operates two Tu-154s leased from Aeroflot. Within twelve months both airliners have carried different company names – Bosnaair, Varda Bosnaair and lately Air VB. Both Tu-154s operate alongside two Yk-42s from their Skopje base.

VIA (VL/VIM)   Bulgaria

Out of Bulgaria's communist shake-out and subsequent privatisation
of their airline industry came Air VIA Bulgarian Airways or Varna
International Airways as originally planned. The airline was
established in 1990 with five new Tu-154Ms in an attractive colour
scheme of purple with stripes and green titles.

The airliners of VIA first appeared in western Europe during the
summer months of 1991 operating holiday charters to the Black Sea
resorts of Varna and Bourgas.

Two of the VIA Tu-154Ms were short-leased to Macedonian Air
Services with titles pending the delivery of their own Palair
Macedonian Tu-154M.